Using Trash

How You Can Rethink, Reuse, Reduce, Recycle, and Rebuild

**DEVELOPED IN COOPERATION
WITH
COSI,
OHIO'S CENTER OF SCIENCE AND INDUSTRY
COLUMBUS, OHIO**

Copyright © 1993 by Scholastic Inc.   All rights reserved. Published by Scholastic Inc.   Printed in the U.S.A.
ISBN 0-590-26138-X
1 2 3 4 5 6 7 8 9 10   09   99 98 97 96 95 94 93 92

ALL PARTS OF AN ENVIRONMENT ARE INTERRELATED; THEREFORE, CHANGES TO ONE PART AFFECT OTHER PARTS.

Using Trash

Through various conservation methods, including recycling, people can control the amount of waste they produce.

Read-Aloud

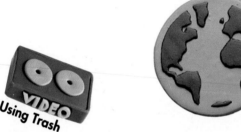

Using Trash

People produce and dispose of waste products in a variety of ways.

Literature

Some methods of waste disposal can damage the environment.

Through rethinking, reusing, and recycling, people can reduce wastes or turn them into useful products.

Literature

What Did We Learn?

What Do People Throw Away?

People make waste where they live, work, and play. What do you think happened here?

Be a garbage detective.

❶ Look around and find some garbage, but don't touch it.

❷ Draw what you find. Tell where you found it.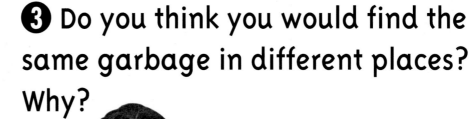

❸ Do you think you would find the same garbage in different places? Why?

THINK!
Can you think of a place where you wouldn't find any garbage?

What Do You Throw Away?

How much garbage does your class make in a day? What kinds of garbage does your class make?

You need:
Bag of garbage
Small plastic bags

Get into garbage.

❶ Look at a mystery bag of things your class threw away. Shake it. Lift it. Poke it. Smell it. What's in the bag?

❷ Now put plastic bags on your hands and open the bag. How can you sort your mystery mess? Try it.

THINK! Can you reuse any of the things you threw away?

How Much Did You Throw Away Today?

Did you find paper in your mystery bag?
How much paper do you think you throw away?

You need:
Paper bag
Masking tape

Measure your paper garbage.

❶ Don't throw away any paper today. Put it in a bag. Take the bag wherever you go.

❷ Open your bag and sort your paper garbage. Count the pieces. How much paper do you throw away in a day?

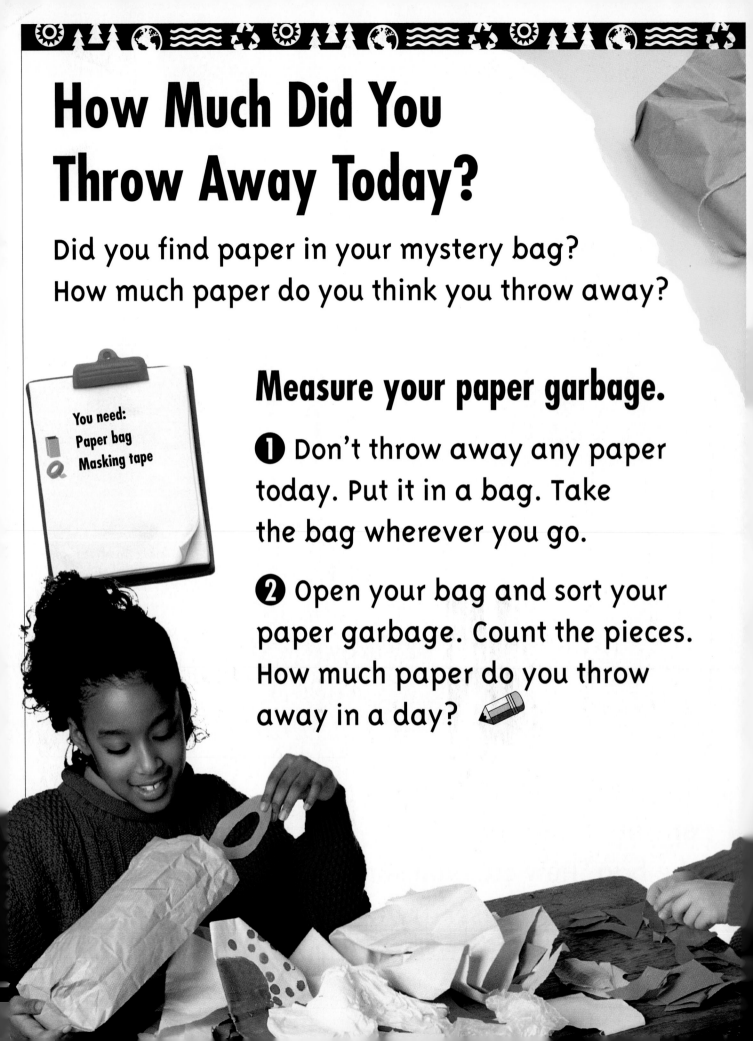

How much paper do you use at home?
How much do you throw away?
Could you throw away less? How?

THINK!
Do you think
you threw away more paper
or more plastic today? How
could you find out?

How Do People Make So Much Garbage?

Did you find packages in your paper garbage? Many packages become garbage very soon after they leave the store.

Look at this picture. Find five things that have more than one package. Are all the packages needed?

You need:
Markers or
crayons

Design some new packages.

❶ Look at the picture. Which packages don't you need? Which packages could you change?

❷ Change this lunch to make less garbage. Draw a picture of the new lunch. ✏️

THINK!
How could you use fewer packages in your own lunch?

How Does Garbage Change?

The things people throw away don't just disappear. Some garbage changes quickly. Some garbage changes slowly. You can test it.

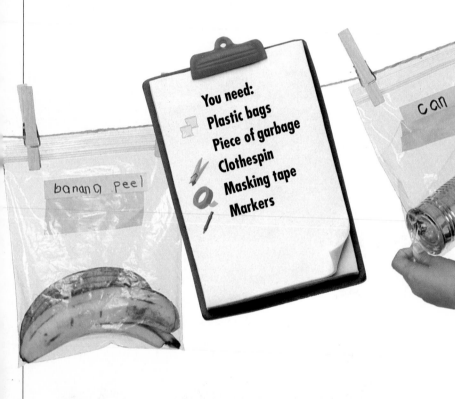

You need:
Plastic bags
Piece of garbage
Clothespin
Masking tape
Markers

banana peel

can

ne
A
S

Make a garbage museum.

❶ Bag your garbage. Label it. Hang it up.

❷ Draw your garbage or write three words to describe it.

❸ Check it every day. What happens?

12

How long do you think it took
for these things to change?

THINK!
What kinds
of garbage
change quickly?

What Happens to Buried Garbage?

Different kinds of garbage change in different ways. Some garbage rots. What is rotting? Which kinds of garbage rot?

You need:
Bottles
Small plastic bags
Dirt
Masking tape
Marker
Garbage
Water
Spoon

Bury some garbage.

❶ Fill the bottles with dirt. Put a different kind of garbage in each bottle. Label them.

❷ Wait three days. Add a little water each day.

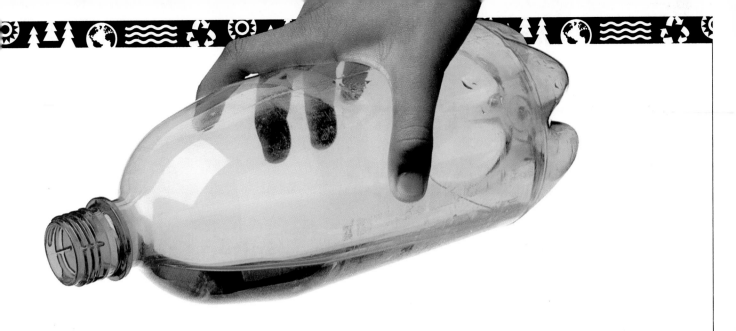

❸ Dig up your garbage. What do you see? What do you smell? Bury it and check it again in three days.

THINK!
What happens to the garbage that doesn't rot?

What Problems Does Garbage Cause?

Every year, each person in the United States throws away about this much garbage. Where does it all go?

Some towns burn their garbage. What does fire burn up? What does fire leave behind?

18 kilograms   580 kilograms

40 pounds   1,227 pounds

Some towns bury their garbage. Towns that bury their garbage use landfills. Do you think everything in a landfill rots?

Where would you find space for a landfill this big?

THINK!
What happens when the landfill is full?

What About Our Oceans?

We're running out of space for landfills.
The oceans are very big and very deep.
What happens if we put garbage in the ocean?

You need:
Clear container
Water
Garbage
Disk
Clay
String
Hand lens

Make your own ocean.

❶ Fill the container with water.
Place your garbage in the water.

❷ Wrap clay around the string.
Put the string through the disk.
Lower the disk into the water.
Stop when you can't see it
anymore.

❸ Predict what will happen
to the water and what
will happen to the garbage.
Check it every day with
your disk and hand lens.

THINK!
How do you think
garbage affects animals
in the ocean?

How Can Garbage Be Used Again?

Instead of throwing things away, people can recycle them. Recycling turns something you have used into something you can use again. Have you used something recycled?
What was it made from?

You need:
- String
- Big boxes
- Garbage

CORN FLAKES

Set up a recycling station.

1 Label boxes for metal, plastic, paper, and things you can use for art projects.

2 Flatten and stack. Wash and sort.

plastic

THINK!
What parts of your garbage can't be recycled?

How Are Food and Plant Wastes Recycled?

Some things we throw away go to a recycling center. But plant and food garbage need to be recycled in a compost pile. Plants and food can rot quickly. Air and water help them rot.

How is a compost pile different from a landfill?

You need:
Box lined with plastic bag
Spoon
Hand lens
Water
Food waste
Leaves or grass
Rocks or twigs
Dirt
Plastic bags

Make some rot.

1 Put dirt between leaves, rocks, and food waste.

2 Stir and add water every day.

3 Wait one week.

What is compost changing into?
How can you use it again?

THINK!
How are leaves recycled in a forest?

How Is Paper Recycled?

Most paper is made from wood. How does using less paper help save trees? How does recycling paper help save trees?

You need:
Used white paper
Hand lens
Plastic cup
Fork
Warm water

Make paper mush.

❶ Tear a used piece of paper into small pieces. Look at a torn edge.

❷ Put the pieces into a cup and cover them with warm water.

❸ Stir the paper to make a wet mush. Pick up some mush. How does it feel?

Paper mush is used to make new paper. What do you think will happen if you squeeze the water out and let it dry?

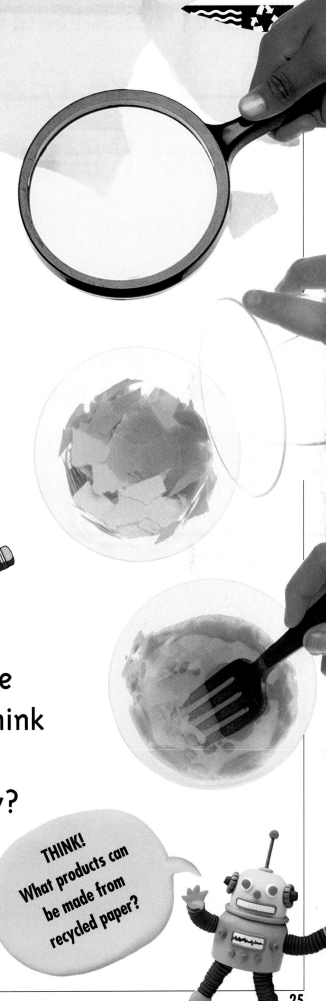

THINK!
What products can be made from recycled paper?

25

How Are Glass and Metal Recycled?

At the recycling center, glass and metal get sorted again. Glass is sorted by color. The green glass goes together to make new green glass.

Metal gets recycled, too. Recycled steel is used in bridges and trains. Recycled aluminum is used in airplanes and bicycles. Sometimes factories sort metal with a magnet.

You need:
Magnet
Metal garbage

Sort metals.

❶ Which things do you think will stick to the magnet? Record your predictions.

❷ Test each object and sort your metal into two piles.

THINK!
What could you store in a used can?

Is It Trash or Treasure?

Recycling is one way to use things again.
Reuse doesn't have to spell W-O-R-K.
You can make it spell F-U-N.

What parts of this playground
used to be garbage?

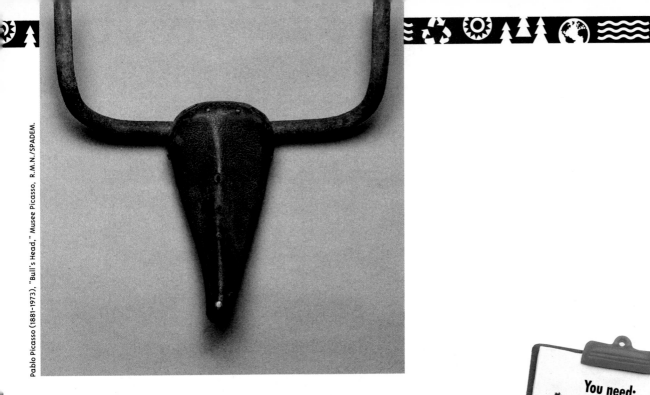

What garbage can you find in these works of art?

You need:
Garbage
Glue
Paint or markers
Scissors
String

Make something new from something used.

❶ Collect some fun garbage. (No food!)

❷ Use your imagination to make something new.

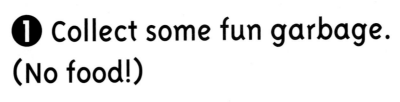

THINK! Why would you want to make art out of trash?

How Can You Help Make Less Garbage?

REUSE

RECYCLE

REDUCE

REBUILD

RETHINK

Think of new ways that you can
recycle, reuse, reduce, and rebuild.

Compost: Plant and food wastes can be recycled in a compost pile. A compost pile needs air and water to change the wastes into fertilizer.

Garbage: Garbage is what people throw away. When people rethink, rebuild, recycle, reduce, and reuse, they make less garbage.

Landfill: A landfill is layers of garbage and clay, soil, or grass. Towns that bury their garbage use landfills.

Package: A package holds and protects something before it is sold. Many packages become garbage soon after they leave a store.

Rebuild: People rebuild when they fix something broken instead of throwing it away.

Recycle: To recycle is to turn old, used objects into different, new things. Garbage must be sorted before it can be recycled.